# About the Author

As a registered nurse who loves literature; I worked throughout the COVID first wave in Intensive Care. My writing reflects my occupation but most significantly my life. COVID19 affected each of our lives. I used poetry to cope with the horrors of the pandemic and also in honour of the amazing doctors and nurses who fought industriously to save each person who became a patient.

Dealing with the suicide of my identical twin has been heart-wrenching, exhausting, but also enlightening. I have penned away at my grief and found some comfort in words. Although I may be lost, I have also found that the most devastating times in our life are, when we are at our most creative – in a raw sense. Bereavement in words, pain and healing in poetry may sum up my work.

Motherhood and life as a parent are something both delightful and terrifying. I try to capture this in words.

Perhaps the detail in my poems will help just one person, because that is how we– as humans – live and love… in detail.

# My Mask

# Rebecca Topham-Roche

# My Mask

Olympia Publishers
*London*

www.olympiapublishers.com
OLYMPIA PAPERBACK EDITION

A CIP catalogue record for this title is
available from the British Library.

ISBN: 978-1-80074-901-6

This is a work of fiction.
Names, characters, places and incidents originate from the writer's
imagination. Any resemblance to actual persons, living or dead, is
purely coincidental.

First Published in 2022

Olympia Publishers
Tallis House
2 Tallis Street
London
EC4Y 0AB

Printed in Great Britain

# Dedication

For, Debs – my beautiful twin

# Acknowledgements

Thank you to my lovely husband, Richard, and 'my little bright', Alfie.

# My Mask

I am not an Intensive Care Nurse
I am just a me
I am not as hard and weathered as I thought
I am actually more horrified than I believed I could be,

I think of the sturdy, tattooed man from last night
I whispered only this morning: "I will see you tonight"
And then I arrived and looked for my hope of hope
But while I was sleeping, he had lost his fight

And deflated, I look over at the soul
In the bed across, tubed and dying
His organs all beaten, betraying him
I am on the verge of crying
But I don't

Instead I listen -and my skin prickles
There is beautiful music here
An Islamic Prayer his mother has asked us to play
They hold the Iphone gently to his ear.
This prayer -it is her touch, her kiss, her 'please live another
day'.

I realise that I am hearing true love transported
His mother's love is tangible; emotive its waves
Her desperate gift of comfort without presence
So heartbreaking a way to end one's days.

To watch a person die alone
Amongst strangers in space suits and masks
This is what rips at my resilience
It is soul destroying, I turn away, pretend to be immersed in
tasks
But I am crying now- and for once- glad of my visor and
mask

# Coughing Kiss

Through the glass window of the Unit

How can the sun be so brightly shining?

Lighting up the pallid, wasting faces

There is real struggle here and dying


It seems a cruel incongruity

That the air out
there is fresh
and clean Whilst
we wear visors
and mumbling
masks

Only a gloved touch to express what our hearts mean


I need to envisage
your smile when you
recover The thought
brings a little bird

like flutter

Because it feels like a
battlefield of tubed and
doomed And the sun out
there just melts hope like
butter


I look at every face and remember

Each is beloved and was busy living before this.

What we may do is limited and desperate

Once downed by this coughing kiss


I have never seen a Consultant wary

Never a 39 year
old tubed, prone
and swollen I have
never seen such a
fight as this
So much this pernicious disease has stolen

# You Are You (COVID)

When I nurse you,

I try to see you

I hear your breath

As I watch your resps

But enough of that

You are not your sats

A person still, forget the ill.


Who are you beneath the pallor,

The skin stretched sallow?


On this bed

The one we all come to dread

You are not a mere task,

I see *you* beneath the oxygen mask

Your skin's deep telling lines

Whisper "once I did" – and betray your times

You liked to laugh,

Someone gave you that.

A thin ring on your finger


Are you as I am?

Who was your man?
Did rose pink play on those lips,

Take excited, wanton sips?

Your sunken eyes may be dull,

But I can envisage their past pull.

Your perfume on the bedside.


Did you ever touch the fluff of hair

On a baby's sweet head with care?

Save and wrap safe – a first tiny tooth,

Rock warmly, sing softly and soothe?

A scribble of a wonky heart is pinned up – over there

Did your cheeks flush in the rush

Or did you possess no less

A resilience, a calm, an enviable hush

Or were you a hothead —

Branded with vigour?

Oh!

Now I guess
that fire was
your
signature
It's there in
your square
jawline.

A child, a girl, a woman, a patient

Such is the transience of life

How can any of us really comprehend?

You are a tapestry, a painting —

Unique in every way until your end.
What did this life give you? What did it take?

Euphoria, achievement, anguish, fear?

I think you have known love,

And still hear its beat echo in your ear

Your pulse dances – sparrow's wrists.


I wish I could read you and

The leathery library of your life,

That grim rattle has halted its writing —

The inevitable roll of time's dice

I am honoured to know you, if only for tonight.


I'm sure you would not choose here

Although we try to make
peaceful – these final
hours Instead,
Think of the sky out there – and the perennial flowers

# If I Should

If I should ever fly so high

Watch me glide – through my eye

You may capture a sparkly day

Appreciate the clouds which play

Around a sun – real with yellow

Watch its descent, quiet and mellow

If I should ever cease to breathe
Take these lungs, ease your wheeze

Inhale deep, stop once and feel

The whoosh of life's newly oiled wheel

Suck in the sweet and also the sour —

Exhale exuberant – you have your hour

If I should ever still forever

And my soul exits with a white feather

Take these bits that would shrivel to dust

Futile to allow such machinery to rust

Envisage the fresh of just one day without wait

For the road's end imaginings and fear to abate.


If I should ever slumber too deep

May you be warmed and gifted to keep

Each and any of these working tools

Before this body quits and cools.

Finally, take happy —

This red heart —

So should I depart… I am soothed at your start.

# Walk Home From Work

There are so many faces

And I remember each one.

Not just today; a decade since —

Or in the month just gone.


If they smile or acknowledge

My mind the image captures.

Cold clay faces, emotionless;

Also set themselves amongst my batches.


I don't miss the little bits so easily

I gaze at wet bubbles on sweaty skin,

And the sloth of stubble

Wonder endlessly at what is within.

The stranger's eye that twitches

A mouth pretty with imperfection

The tiny hairs on a balding head

A nose that grows in an odd direction.


They pass me in the street

And my eyes sharpen on those ears

Aren't they a strange shape?

Rare doorways from which he hears.


What makes her happy?

Woman with shiny mirror of hair?

She looks fab enough to party and shag

Or is her diary bare?


Is that man over there mourning?
He doesn't raise his poor head

'I'm not grieving or sad, just pissed off,'

His shoulders just sullenly said.

Buying milk, I study the security guard

He thinks it's a calculated flirting

So I can swipe some a block of cheese

The age old tactic of diverting.

And so how will I seize them all?

Note each amazing peculiarity

With my love for detail

There is such an abundance of singularity.

# Night Shift

Waiting for the night shift

Is like waiting to die

The sun is blazing

And I want to cry.


Voices high and fervent;

Summer has appeared.

I can hear the shrill laughter;

Kebab BBQs being seared.


I'm a miserable miser

And I so envy their fun
I think only of the drudgery

Before the shift has even begun.

Should be grateful I'm here

Happy and blessed

A job secretly loved

Though I'm hot and stressed.


My lovely, tanned soul mate

And sweet chinned little boy

Will play in the warm evening

My jealousy is a playful ploy.


Because really it's nice to be there,

When most are mid dream

To be a focused shadow

Things aren't always as they seem.


Patients who stir and wander

Can't sleep in the heat

They tell us fantastical stories

Role and personality meet.


There are beeps of IVACS

And the echo of unsynced snores.

Time to listen with intent —

Revelations only darkness implores.


The girl whose given history

Is missing the significant past;

She may disclose her fears

And we can help at last.


It's so often the blackness;

The paradoxical comfort of night

That lends some patients the spur

To divulge the despair they fight.

# Grief

**Loss of You – Mental Health Awareness**

There isn't a magical spell

But the there is a story to tell

The great story of your life

You didn't always live on the edge of a knife


It wasn't always so

You loved the
snow and to hear
the wind blow You
relished a run in
sheets of rain
Running made you strong, pounding away pain


You once loved with ferocity, gentle still

I have the pictures

you drew on my
windowsill Your life
was not easy, you
were often afraid
This was from trauma, not just how you were made


You survived so long
where many would have
died If they lived as we
had; and you so rarely
cried.

I know more than any,
that you tried, you tried
Life was too much for
your soul to abide


I am so angry you left me

But just perhaps I can be

Grief is not just salty tears

When you have loved for years and years.


You were ill for just over a year

And I watched you disappear

Into yourself, out of yourself

I look at your picture on my white shelf


Mental Health Awareness month – October

I want everyone to
know that for you
it is over You
should be here –
under the waning
sun

Let others know and not judge what childhood trauma has
done.

# If I Could Write You a Rainbow

If I could write you a rainbow

And make you smile

Put the colour back in your eyes
Make you happy for a while


If I could catch the elusive feather

Let you stroke it in your hand

Remind you of the satisfaction

Of the flow of white, powdery sand


If I could let you feel the wind again

Let it – on your bare face – blow

See the sparkle of a million diamonds

In the respite of fresh snow

If I could take away the fear

Open your curtains to the good

The lighter part of this life

The love hearts carved in wood


If I could let you know true love again

How it hides in many ways

Let you really see what we felt for you

Before you ended your days

I would, I would, I would

# Whilst I am Alive

Whilst I am alive

I shall lucidly remember
The journey of these two years

It began in November.


You lost your way

Became so ill

I wish I could change it

That you were here still


Whilst I am alive

I shall live with regret

That I could not help you

I cannot forget.

You were desperate –

To heal and be well

I know that

Whilst myself – I also fell


Whilst I am alive

I shall live these years

With you silently beside me

Fighting grief and fears


You were my twin

You were – to me – everything

Let me hear you laugh

Let me hear you sing

# For My Bright

I forgot what it felt like

To run my fingers along a silvery wall

Wet with fresh rain

After a monumental fall.

And to see the sparkle

Of the sun on our lake

Watch a mother with her ducklings

And the watery patterns in their wake

I forgot the comforting quiet

Of the middle of the night

When all are slumbering

And the moon is the street's only light.

And the pale blossom petals

Floating like pink snow

Decorating the pavement

And my hair with a bow.

I forgot to look at you

Appreciate the colour in your eyes

I forgot you loved me

And that our love never dies.

And yet here you are

Your face so very near

May I keep you forever

In my heart... just here

4/7/21

# Look Closely and I Am There

I am the sunset when day is done

I am the laughter in your son


I am in the twist of the old oak tree

Touch its trunk and you will feel me.


I am in the song of the rainbow of birds

I am alive in each of your words


I am there – in the night sky –

A star that shoots bright and high


I am the solitary white snow feather
You are not alone… we pick it up together


I am in the sunbeam's gentle ray

I never left you… I never went away.

# My Twin

My twin – she arrived head first,

Me feet first, last.

Thirty-two minutes apart

Not so very fast.


Through DNA's dictation

Exact voice, hair, eyes

My very first love

My very first disguise


We see the other's insides

As we know our very own

We are each the other's self

Biological clone.

Contrasting inclinations

Myself, I love my men

She loves her women

Not so alike there, then.


We are a shifting breeze
Without her, no me

Without me, no her

Is this how it's meant to be?


She is my backbone

When mine's all chalk

I am her voice

When she's afraid to talk.


We are yin and yang

Ferocious friends

Even worse enemies

But each and all mends.


Fate was generous.

A world together

A face as mirror.

And love forever.

# She Knows

I know she knows

She is telling me to keep going

I know it by the magical tinkle

Of the wind-chime blowing


I know she knows
By the white feather

Tossed carelessly on the dusty path

In this summer weather


I know she knows

As she walks silently

Through the trees with me

Hoping for a break of sunshine

So that it is her I see

I know she knows

When I walk down the hospital corridor

That I see her little determined frame

And that this mind's eye of mine –

Envisages her smile the same

I know she knows

How much I wish her here

Sat in that tiny scarlet chair.

With laughter and tear

I know she knows

I am struggling to live

Without her.

She would want me to live.

And remember the best of her
24/6/21

41

# Beloved Face

Today I laughed myself —

Right through the sad

Relied on facade

Is that so bad?


To stay busy

Like an actual bee

Despite the raw pain

Inside of me


I keep seeing your face

When I look over there

Into the bathroom's mirror

Magnifying my despair

But I saw you smile

I saw your shoulders relax

I know in my soul

That you chose not to come back


You were stolen away

To a sweeter place

I stroke your cheek in our picture

Touch your beloved face

# My Wish

Scattered, hidden stealthily

I saw a hundred wishes today.

Just one would be enough

To see you smile and hear you say:


*"After all these years of struggle*

*I really found it here at last*

*A release from the grind*

*Even though my life passed too fast.*


*I reached and touched peace*

*I am beautifully devoid of worry*

*Though I know you love me*

*And for my loss you will be forever sorry,"*

I see you at peace

Your lovely face in my mind's eye

You caught
my wish in
weightless
hands And
carried it up
high into the
bluest sky


17/8/21

# You Always Loved This Place

Do you remember when we sat –

On this crooked bench together?
I look down at my muddy boots.

And glimpse a white feather.


So now I see you came.

Settling yourself on the bench's wood

Next to my heart and longing

The grass, trees and the mud.


I know you feel the space;

It's so languidly liberating

You can see the ragged grassy mounds

And our familiar walk waiting.

The silhouette of wavy hills

Where – in sun – you could have lain.

Now swampy and flattened with water

From last night's summer rain.


The birds make silly squawks

And behind us is hidden our lake

Where we often indulged in story;

Admired the ducklings' military wake


It's more pretty than you remember

The trees have found their grace

Growing in silver twists and turns

You always loved this place.


When I sit here quietly

I know your loss with a raw regret

Nature was ever your beloved balm

And here... I can never forget

# I came from here

I came from here

From a windy, textile town

I came from the trees

Where the leaves flutter down


I came from one egg

I came here as two

I came here wearing red

Whilst she always wore blue


I came from a granite city

From a coarse, crude farm

I came from darkness

Rested in resentful arms

I came here with a smile —

Even those days could not steal —

I came here with dreams

With hands holding zeal

I came here and learnt:

This is a cruel, beautiful place

The pain of raw love

Now etched upon my face

I came here to live

## "We Had The Hours"

Sometimes I think that is you I see

At the turn of this leafy street

Same walk and tilt of head

Determined stride of feet.


Sometimes I think that it is you I hear

Laughing in the shifting breeze

Or your silhouette pass peacefully

Between the silver trunk of trees


Sometimes I think I could touch you

Link my arm – familiar – through yours
Walk with you when the weather is wild

And the wind screams and roars

Always I wish for just one more hour

I would do anything, anything, anything

To see your beloved face again

And feel the absolute elation it would bring


"We had the hours,"

We weren't allotted anymore

Life came and stole you from us

And gently closed that door

# Please Hear

I am aware that I've shared

The dark side of grief

But this is the positive

Please hear me speak

For her to leave

Felt like a blunt gunshot –

I am not here to glamorise

The things I am not

I look around me

And here is my gold
My son, my husband

Fab friends of new and of old


The thing with this pain

Is that I get to choose;

If I let it destroy me

If I resign myself to lose


I have a beautiful life

I am unbelievably thankful for that


Healing at last just maybe —

As I sit where I have never sat


So please see me as me

I didn't plan for this horror

But now I am able to appreciate

My lovely life and my tomorrow

# Life

# Bewitched

The lazy hours were mine

Routine a bitch to follow.

Ticking clocks ticked

A bed warm but hollow

With languid imprint
Of freedom's idle bind.

Seldom thoughts of future

Just the transient kind.


Only appointments managed

Were shifts for the dosh;

And those with my mates

To gorge booze and nosh.

No intention to clean house

Or feed another's needs –

Makeup and music

Flash of last night's deeds.


No school run to heed

Or dog to walk

Mobile and messaging

And gossipy talk.

A fridge home for wine

Not milk, cheese and ham

Sleeping and partying.

Now just an echo of who I am


Never once imagined

A calendar would hang there.

Or wellies for dog walking

Would stand by the stair.

That a little blue room
Should appear with its toys

And that my life would buzz loudly

With a happier noise.


That steps up a path

And bark of a dog

Would rouse satisfied signal

Of a husbandly snog.

That I would have cooked

Food edible for three.

Shared the bits and the bounce

I always kept for me.


That a sweaty little human

Should sit in that chair

Talking sweet nonsense

And the depth I would care.


It's all alien to me

How I travelled whole here

Bewitched with utter normality

And that I would hold it so dear.

# Magic of Life

I long to touch you

Trace my finger along your skin
Look into your eyes

And feel the magic within

Magic which makes the sky sparkle

On a clear winter's night

Feel the wind gently guide me

From darkness into light

Magic that makes memory

Crinkly pages in a metaphorical book

With spells to live this life by

I close my eyes and look

And there it is – I see it!

Magic scattered everywhere

In the greenness of the grass

In the Autumn in your hair


In the waning sun's caress

In the laughter of a babe

And whether or not I know it

I stand in Aladdin's golden cave

# That Apple

I shall begin with lemon

To zest my green tea.
  Eat egg white omelette

Take vitamin B


Eye that apple

With smug delight

Polish its skin

Take a self righteous bite.


Squat fifty times

With practised ease

Staunch in purpose

Complete one-hundred burpees.

Triumph five miles

Unperturbed by the wet

Strong and determined

Sexy sweat.


Open my eyelids

And stare at the wall

Look down at my belly

No definition at all.


Arrive in the kitchen

Shoot caffeine with glee

Swirl in the blue top

Ignore the fat free.


Have a leisurely vape

Fruity and strong

Wolf old chocolate buttons

Yeah! cheating is wrong.


Tomorrow I will nail it;

Become a juicing expert

Go green gracefully

Become teeny and pert.


Footfall on the stairs

Is the love of my life.

Buttons are bulldozed

And that apple... beneath the knife

# Fat

Oh to have a toned, tapered tummy

A tiny ballerina's waist

I inspect for
cellulite,
new rolls of
fat Vain
minutes of
agony I
painfully
waste.


What do we really achieve

In this torturous pursuit to be thin?

Health is wealth but does *skinny*

Really reflect what's within?
Will my IQ rocket

Or will I acquire new tongues?

Will my blood turn liquid gold

Diamonds exhale from my lungs?

What a load of shite;

This self flagellation

I am stupid enough to enlist

Like most women of this nation.

I will still be me

Fat bird or starving wing

So I'm withdrawing my entry

I don't need to win.

# Our Sad Tree

Let's sit together beneath the apple tree

Yes I know she's now bare

But I understand

Look at her arms outstretched with care.


An old rusty
wind-chime
struggles up there
A begrudging
tinkle, blemished
bark

And what do you think
– my lovely ginger bear–
Your climbing frame
now so stark?
Go on! Run up that bark, along a branch

Make her feel useful, loved and needed

I'm not coming with you. Not a chance!

I'm sitting here, with the dandelions I should have weeded


You have inquisitive eyes, Billy, a loud meow

We must care for our despondent apple tree

Even if we don't really know how.

Maybe we can remind her of what she can be?


Apples buffed red with crimson gloss

She was beautiful, motherly – wasn't she Billy?

Peering down through boney branch

His eyes are disdainful, he thinks this human is silly.


Talking to a cat and an apple tree

Madness – for sure – is this!

But sat here, I make us a wish:

*"You will get back to yourself, I promise,"*

You are still sturdy despite
the weather's missiles We
have a lot in common you
and I

We are proud; hiding
behind sun-rays and
smiles Billy – bored –
leaps into the sky
So now, it's just you and me – dear apple tree –

When I lost myself, you were losing too

I watched you everyday, I could see

Your lovely apples falling – and what it did to you.


But together we can fix each other

Seasons are transient, loss
can sometimes be gain
There will be more apples,
one after another

And when they are red, my cheeks – too – shall be pink
again.

# Real Gold

Today I arrived early

I stretched my neck, longer than long

Glimpsed his profile in the glass corridor

Captured him skipping blithely along.

And then down the curly steps

To the crowded noisy door.

His teacher smiling and at pleasing ease

In the midst of screech, whoops and roar

I have a chocolate coin for him

Token of guilt – wrapped in real gold

He isn't wearing jumper or coat

Although it's crispy cold.

And when I insist he wear them

He is snappy and loathe to agree

I am firm and he relents

But there is no Alfie kiss for me.


I have missed him so much.

Spent such intense hours with them –

Strangers with illness or injury –

They are my grind; but my son is my gem.


Why do we have to do this

Be mums, but only a snatch at a time?

Perfect role model, do
and be everything at
once career, teatime,
playtime, homework and
bedtime.


I feel like stealing away for a day or forever

Those teachers see him more than me

Call in sick at bloodbath work

Stolen hours together, little him and me.


If it was seventy years ago

I could be standing here
with contrasting dreams A
snotty baby snug on my
hip

Pining for escape from nappies and stitching seams
Never happy, although we women have it all?

Freedom, career, family – a validated voice

Careers may blossom for decades; fertility cannot

But I feel faint regret – in the sequence of my choice

# Free

A few more days of this bleak January

And we shall see the wild, sweet sea

Watch land become a map from our balcony

And forget – for a time – what came to be.


From indescribable pain – a pivotal flee.

A gift, an escape, a chance to just be

How else to retain some sanity –

Than to sit together beneath a palm tree?


Engulfed in water – warm and salty

Who cares if my wound stings with intensity?

Let me find acceptance in the perennial folds of sea.

I so ache to float there – light, guiltless – and be free

# Summer Sun

Do you know how much I've missed you

Since you stealthily skipped away?

Your scent and colours illustrious

Flowers like jewels, sparkling through the day

I miss the burns you left behind

On the grass through the patio doors

And how you lingered during the evening

Generously painting the fences and floors.

And the way people just sat and smiled

When you went down like a drunk

All forgotten and forgivable

Despite how low you sunk.

I miss your warm body

How it fits so snug against mine

Lying beneath you ecstatic

Laughing and drinking wine.


Bare legs and arms,

I remember the flowers on the apple tree

Sitting beneath with the dandelions

Thinking 'I really am free'

# First Love

You never returned

My eyes looked for years.

The being I loved sweet

In my mind appears.
Loving finds fable

As the claw of culture

Swoops down and devours –

Such a heartless vulture.


And then you went away

Back to your past

A brooding intelligence

You saw beneath the mask

Espying my weakness

Even before it had grown.

I think you saw it then

The seeds my blood had sown.


You tried to help me

Retrospection speaks now

Curb my excesses,

I was too stupid to learn how.


Yet you collected my years –

A painted, popped up soul –

Played like game.

Time and tenderness stole.


What would I do

To relive those hours?
Reach up to you again

Be entwining flowers?

Nothing

Not even memory's gloss deters.

The love I have for my boys

Indescribable in words.

# Daughter of Addiction

Tomorrow at dawn, she shall open her eyes wide

Sit up, take responsibility and know that her mind's eye lied

A mirage where she wore
a bright red wine stain As
a tattoo around the lips...
was the artist to blame?

Perhaps in this story – she had
scattered around her the tools
To feel peace, to refrain from the soak
of the intoxicating pools

Of the liquid which drowned him, the
horrors that came to pass. Colour, creed,
culture or class – do not decide the drinker of
the glass

She missed the signs, allowed her
person to become entwined With him

whose dear face appeared in every
glass of wine


A child of addiction, lucky – this one –
to finally learn who she is That those
penalties were not hers, but nor were
they his


Though she loves him still – now with
forgiveness' tame pain – *We are not
fated by our nurture,* our ends will not be
the same

# Children's

**Do You See?**

Look up at the moon

How it shines like a safe silver nest

This is your light in darkness

This is rest


Hear the wind outside?

This is a music to savour

Whoosh, moan, whoosh

This is nature


Watch the autumn leaves

How wistfully away they blow

This is poignant farewell

This is letting go.

Stroke her fur

See how she gazes, so fond

This is unfeigned devotion

This is bond

Study your pearly nails

How lovingly they are trimmed

This is how we care in detail

This is nurturing

See that photo?

Smiling three by the sea

This is happiness captured

This is our memory

Place your cheek to my chest

Hear it?

*Beat, beat, beat*

This is our life

This is where love meets.

# Storm's Story

Let's tell a story

One that's gory

Look from the window

See the street below?


Wind tears with teeth

Malevolent thief

Of eyeballs

And shawls
Of hair sleek

Woe for the weak

Whilst a gusty Goliath

Revels in this riot

Stamping speed

At demon's heed

Stealing away

Humans today

Mere dolls flying high

No sweet goodbye


Trees like bone

Snap crack with moan

And rain a sharp knife

Disdain for life

Sheets of it smother

One after another


Hide in the house

Without even a mouse

Hear the creak?

In it sneaks…

Whirls and waits

Growls and grates

Goose-pimple fear
It's so very near.

Dead soul of storm

No more warm

Cold like corpse

In it walks…

# Your Fairytale

See that paving stone over there

Beneath the wall's stern side –

Where we often walked hand in hand by?

There, I'm afraid, a fragile fairy died.


See how it remains matt and dull

Even as the days become bright and fine?

No sparkle – stone still

Just another tread of the road's monotonous line.


See that old shop – closed and bare –

Its windows boarded, sad and wan?

Once there was green chocolate sold there

By that kindly, odd "green chocolate man."

One hot summer
there was a
miniature house
Crudely painted
for raucous pixies
to meet – (Now
empty, faded,
quiet as a mouse)

The rent, remember, they paid to you – a shiny daily sweet.


But one dry Wednesday morning – you woke up older

You mused and frowned and stopped believing

Fading faith in fairytale; the dragon's fire colder.

It was *then* that the fragile fairy ceased breathing.

# Alfie's Lockdown Talisman

In the darkness of this January

When there is so much

Which we do not know

Respite arrives – silent –

In a blanket of white snow


Footprints appear

Human, feline and canine

Black indents
where there
were none
before Disease
may be all
around us
Yet I feel a warm swirl as I watch the boys I adore


I am excited to hear Alfie's dirty laugh

As always – he refuses gloves

With the world as it is on this very day.

Utter normality becomes exquisite

And there is a charm in his pink fingered play


He shall be freezing later

A formidable snowman is on the cards
Let's ignore the
daily smother of
this disease A
child only once in
this knife of a
life

No more fear, let him have this sweet reprieve


His snowman is grand where he stands

Perhaps six foot tall,

I somehow see him as a sort of talisman

Owning the front square of garden

Where his transient life – by Alfie – began

Through the curtain I peep again

A life patted together by my beloved child

He will stay upright a while if any luck

That snowman is made of different stuff,

He has a smug, laid back look.

Today he is a day old – well, almost

Some thief has stolen his nose!

Still proud though, without moan or sound

Alfie will feed his nose a new crooked carrot

And his buttoned belly will become icy round.

Oh, to forget a world in these white hours!

My lips curve

Suddenly happy – with an innate knowing:

Our boy has freedom and play

I look outside again… and hooray! It is snowing!

15/1/21

# Boy

I have held many hands

But yours was the warmest

Possessive little grip

When life was at its starkest


I have kissed many cheeks

Round, porcelain, pink

Yet, I know yours so well –

Their shape could be marked in ink.


I have loved so many

Given them my red heart

But it is yours I know the rhythm of –

I was there at its start

And so here are the bones of me

Where my strength and weaknesses lay

With this sweaty, muddy, laughing boy

Who gallops bright throughout my day